HIDDEN DEPTHS

FROM AUTOSTEREOGRAM TO HYPERVISION

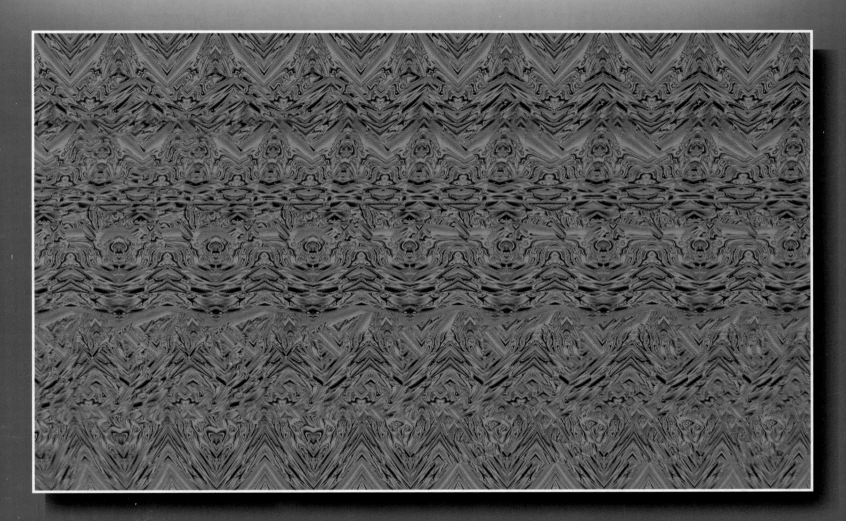

COMPILED BY HARRY STOREY • TEXT BY RICHARD GIRLING

STUDIO EDITIONS

Acknowledgements

It was stated when I first got involved with autostereograms that they were like snake oil – you believe snake oil works but have no proof! With autostereograms, you don't believe they work, but they really do!

My gratitude to the following people who all managed to reach hypersight with no hindsight! To my wife Roz, for her research and patience; to my daughter Nicki who introduced me to this artform; and to my son Dan for teaching me hypersight. To Dan Robinson for his brilliant colour interpretation; to Sonia Land who made the whole project possible through her tremendous enthusiasm, AND reached five levels of hypersight!; to Stephanie Lloyd who pulled it all together with great panache; and to Richard Girling for his excellent written interpretation of our research.

Finally, my gratitude to three very important individuals: to Dave Eichorst, Director, Lookinglass creations, inc., Fort Worth, Texas, USA, for allowing us to use his very imaginative and artistic work; to Christopher Tyler, Associate Director, Smith-Kettlewell Eye Research Institute, San Francisco, USA, who started this whole 3D phenomenon; and to Dr Brian Rogers, Dept. of Experimental Psychology, University of Oxford, UK (for technical advice on random-dot techniques). Thank you all!

Harry Storey, 1994

This edition first published in 1994 by Studio Editions Ltd,
Princess House, 50 Eastcastle Street, London W1N 7AP, England

The right of Harry Storey to be identified as the Author of this Work has been asserted
in accordance with the Copyrights, Designs and Patents Act 1988.

ISBN 1 85891 230 X
Printed in Singapore

Contents

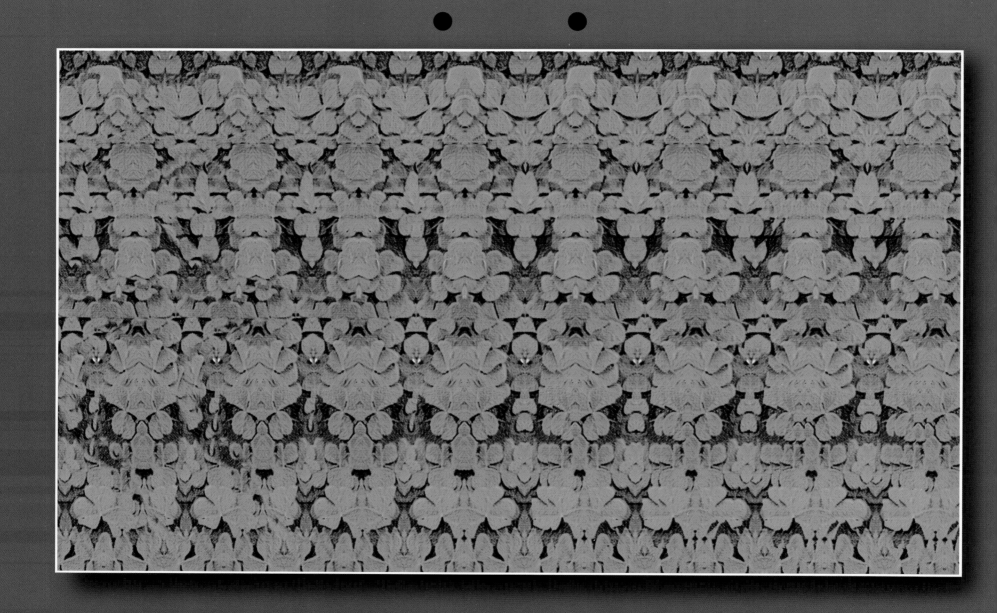

The Story of the Autostereogram

Let us begin by imagining something that could never happen.

You are sitting alone in a room, staring at the wallpaper. As you sit, you feel an odd, slightly dizzying sensation. It is unsettling, but not unpleasant. You feel as if you are beginning to lose your grip on the reality of the room around you, as if your mind is being separated from your body. The patterns on the wallpaper have a strange fluidity about them; they no longer seem quite flat. The bands of colour are rippling like fish under water, and you are losing your sense of distance.

Suddenly, the rippling stops. The wall swims away to leave a glassy void of infinite space. Within the void appears a cloud. Then another, and another. Beneath the clouds you can see strange creatures suspended in space. They do not resemble any creatures you have seen before. They look like something from a storybook, or a dream, and yet they are as solid and real-looking as the wall they have replaced. From behind them appear others, then more and more until the sky is filled with them, rank upon rank, stretching to a horizon too far away to see.

You look away for a second, and when you look back, they are gone. In their place is the wall again, solid plaster and brick, with its bizarrely patterned wallpaper.

No, you have not been invited to imagine the effect of swallowing an hallucinogenic drug! And yes, it is true, you *have* been misled – though only very slightly. In all the above, the only truly misleading sentence was the first.

This is not 'something that could never happen'. Indeed, it is very similar to what *will* happen when you turn the pages of this book. But although you have only a sheet of paper, instead of a wall, be prepared: these are some of the most remarkable sheets of paper ever made. The scientific name for them is *autostereograms*. The technique for producing them has been developed over the last decade in the USA, and they demonstrate one of the most extraordinary conjuring tricks that optical science has ever played on the human eye.

All the visual information that your brain needs to 'see' a complete 3-D picture is printed on a flat surface – virtual reality on a bookplate. That in itself would be remarkable enough. But it doesn't end there. The images can be viewed in more than one way. Different viewers will see different perspectives and depths. The same person could see different things on different days. What is distant on one day could be crystal clear on the next: it is, quite literally, all a matter of *focus*.

You don't need a lens or other special viewing device to enjoy an autostereogram. You *do* have to master a simple technique for focusing your eyes, but it should take no more than a few minutes to practise and perfect. You will find an easy, step-by-step guide to it on page 42. A very small minority of people have visual defects which make it difficult for them to see autostereograms. To reassure yourself that you are not one of them, try this simple test. Hold your index fingers tip to tip, about a quarter of an inch apart and three inches in front of your nose. Focus your eyes beyond them on an object across the room, and you should be able to see an image of a third finger floating between your fingertips.

Some people fancy that the resulting image looks like a sausage – hence it is called the 'Hot Dog Test'. If you move your fingers slightly apart, you will see the 'floating' hot dog.

If you can do this test, and it is at least 90 per cent certain that you can – then it follows that you have stereoscopic vision, and will be able to 'read' autostereograms.

The technique for focusing your eyes at will, either behind or in front of the page (just as you focused them behind your fingers), is central to the way autostereograms work.

'Hallucinogenic' wallpaper is one possible way in which we may entertain ourselves with autostereograms in the future. But it will not be the first time that 3-D, or *stereoscopic*, effects have been noticed in drawing-room walls. Indeed, wallpaper played an important part in the way stereoscopic vision came to be understood. Without it, there might have been no autostereograms at all.

The autostereogram on page 7 is an example of a repetitive pattern often found in wallpaper designs. Keep staring at the pattern and, after some 45 seconds or so, the horizontal and vertical lines will separate from the background and appear to float towards you.

A Scottish physicist, Sir David Brewster, was the first man to officially record an out-of-mind experience brought about by his wallpaper. In 1844, he noticed that if he stared at the small repetitive pattern on his wall for long enough, he could produce an illusory stereoscopic effect. The patterns seemed to shift, and then to settle again at a different depth, as if the wall had suddenly moved towards him.

The discovery led Brewster to write several scientific papers that contributed a great deal to our understanding of stereoscopic vision. It was also (though he could not have known it at the time) a key observation that would lead, 140 years later, to the development of the autostereogram.

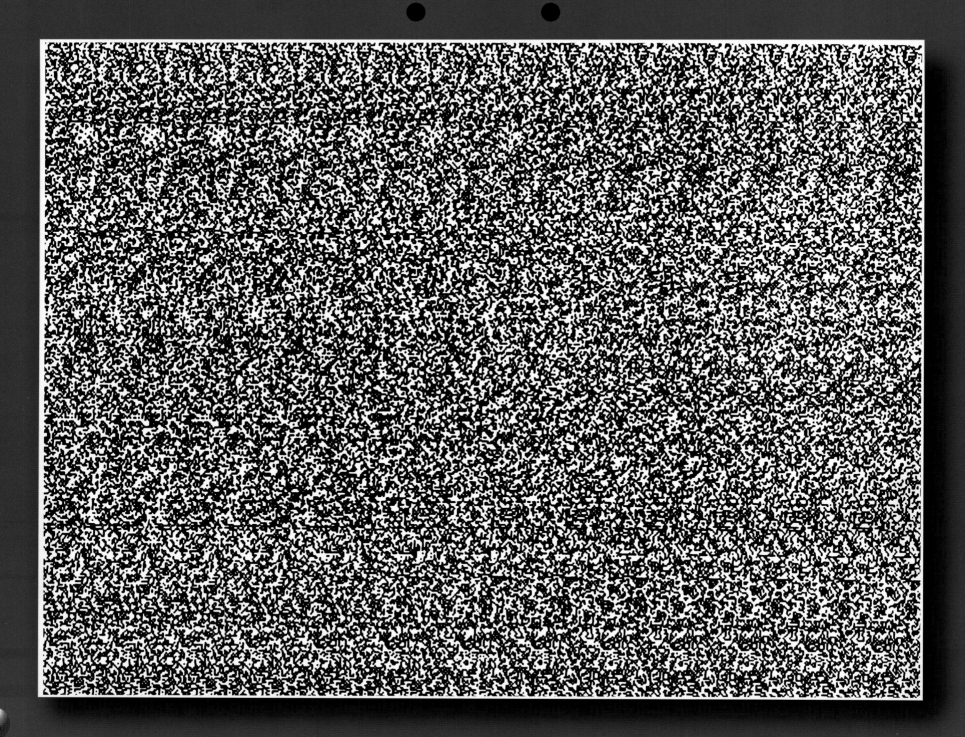

To understand stereoscopic vision, try another simple experiment with your finger held up about three inches in front of your nose. If you keep both eyes open, you will notice that no part of the room behind the finger is obscured. There is a floating 'shadow' of a finger, but it is as if you can see straight through it to the scene beyond. If you now open and close your eyes alternately, you will notice two things. First, the finger *does* now obscure part of the view. Second, the finger appears to move relative to your nose as you change from eye to eye (an effect known to science, not unsurprisingly, as 'nasal shift').

This is a crude but effective demonstration of the crucial difference between normal binocular (two-eyed) and monocular (one-eyed) vision. In binocular vision it is the different angles of view from your two eyes that allow you to see around the upraised finger, and which create the 3-D 'pictures' in your brain. The two eyes, working in tandem, calculate the relative 'depth' (i.e distance from the eye) of different objects inside the field of vision. The nearer you are to an object, the more acutely will your eyes converge to focus on it.

These perceptions of depth are the building blocks of any 3-D image, and all stereoscopic techniques in the past (3-D photography, for example) have mimicked the eyes by using paired lenses set a small distance apart. Children's 'Viewmaster' toys work on exactly this principle, which was first demonstrated by Charles Wheatstone in 1836 when he made his 'stereoscope' – the world's first 3-D viewing device.

The Wheatstone stereoscope used paired mirrors, set at an angle of 45 degrees to each eye, to combine two simple line drawings into a single 3-D image. Until very recently, all stereographic images had been achieved in much the same way, by using two separate, slightly different but easily recognisable 'monocular' images, which – unlike autostereograms – can be recombined into a 3-D picture only through the use of lenses or mirrors. This does not mean, of course, that they have no special value of their own. A version of the Wheatstone stereogram is still used for diagnosing eye defects, though mirrors now tend to reflect computer-generated images rather than drawings or photographs.

Stereoscopic photographic techniques have had a further important function. In World War II, photographic reconnaissance aircraft used twinned cameras to reveal the positions of camouflaged ground installations. Whereas skilfully camouflaged guns, aircraft and buildings would merge invisibly into the background of an ordinary photograph, they stood out with total clarity when snapped by paired lenses in 3-D. This technique is still used extensively in modern aerial surveillance.

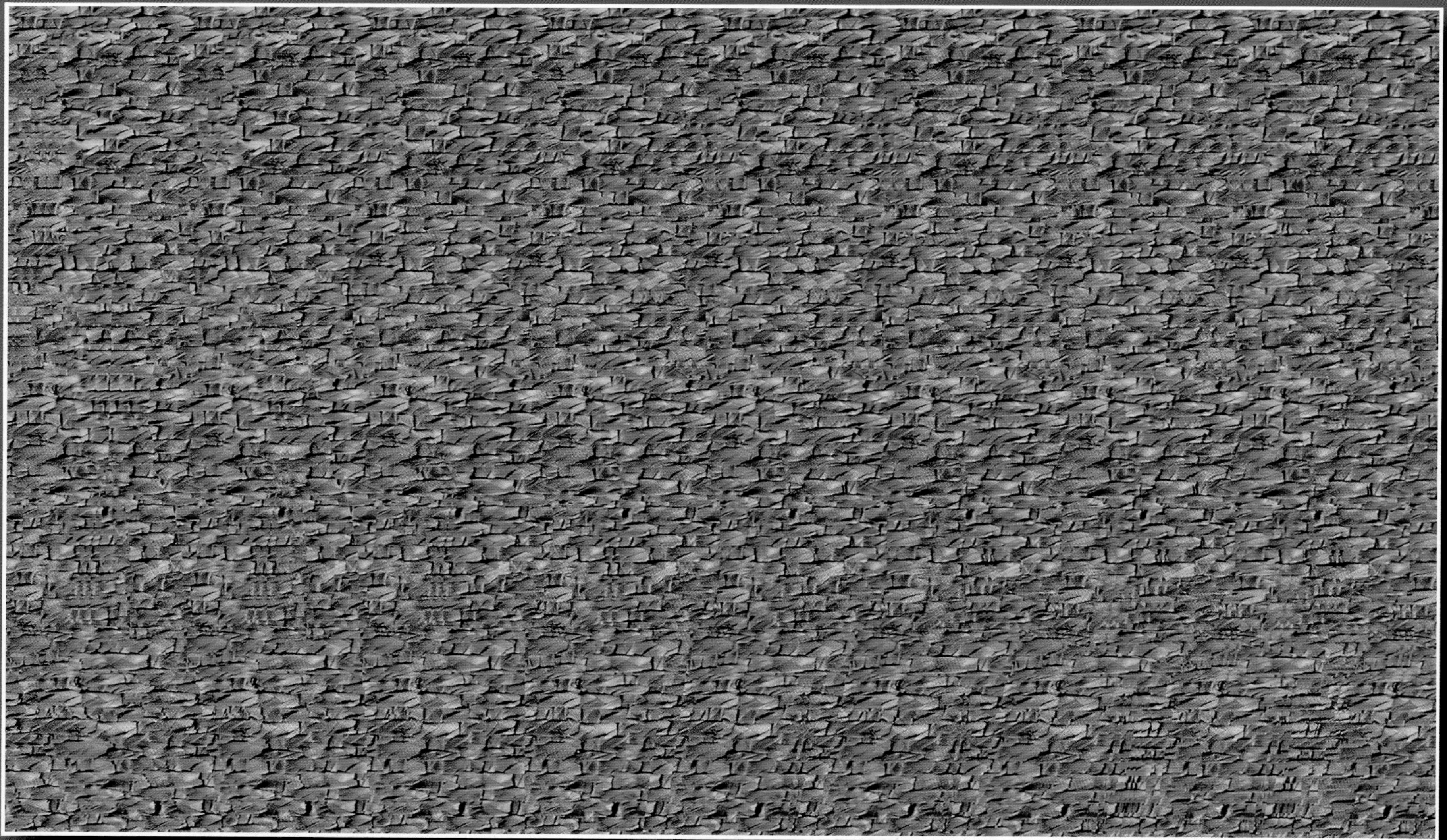

Trickery of the Brain

The long-term importance of Sir David Brewster's observations concerning wallpaper – the 'wallpaper effect' – was its demonstration of the brain's capacity to trick itself (though Brewster himself thought it was all a matter of eye movement, rather than something that happened in the brain). The diagrams on pages 12 and 13 show you how it works.

The three diagrams on page 13 show three different ways of looking at a section of vertically-striped wallpaper. (To help you to follow the explanation, the stripes have been numbered A, B and C.)

Diagram 1 on page 13 shows what happens when both eyes are focused on the middle stripe (B) on page 12. This is the normal binocular view, and results in the brain 'placing' the stripe exactly on the plane of the wall. In other words, you see it where it is.

Still looking at the striped wallpaper on page 12, cross your eyes slightly. Your left eye now sees stripe C. Your right eye sees stripe A. (You will therefore see stripes A, AB, BC, C). Your brain is immediately bamboozled. It expects to combine the two similar monocular images into a single stereoscopic picture, and that's exactly what it now succeeds in doing. It merges the two identical stripes and 'sees' them as one.

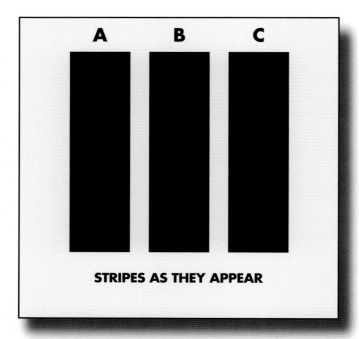

STRIPES AS THEY APPEAR

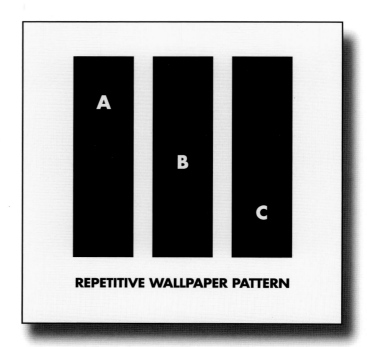

REPETITIVE WALLPAPER PATTERN

Notice that the eyes' point of focus (the point where the two sight-lines intersect), is no longer on the plane of the wall, but *in front of it*. This is where the brain now 'sees' the stripe, with the effect that the wall now appears to have advanced towards the viewer. This is convergent viewing.

Diagram 3 shows what happens if you uncross your eyes and diverge focus. You do this by looking beyond or through the middle stripe. Your left eye now sees stripe A, your right eye sees stripe C, and you yourself will see stripes A, AB, BC and C. A fourth stripe has now appeared; your confused brain still requires a single image, and so it makes sure it gets one. This time, however, the point of focus, and the apparent position of the stripe, is *behind* the plane of the wall, which will now appear to have moved backwards.

In scientific terms, the effects described in Diagrams 2 and 3 are called 'Convergent' and 'Divergent' vision. They are essential to the way autostereograms work, and you will find the techniques for using them described on page 42. As the effect – whether convergent or divergent –

will be uniform whichever part of the wall you look at, the illusion is of the whole wall being displaced, or of *moving* if you readjust your focus.

Of course, the 'wallpaper effect' depends on *regular* vertical patterns. When stripes are *irregular* and multi-directional, the result can cause a serious sense of disturbance as the brain wrestles in vain to make order out of chaos. Anyone who has viewed the work of the abstract painter Bridget Riley will know the feeling.

The 'wallpaper effect' has been noted wherever tiny patterns are endlessly repeated. Knitters of Fair Isle pullovers, for example, have seen their patterns suddenly leap out at them like holograms. People viewing ancient tribal artworks in Central and Southern America have experienced very similar hallucinatory effects.

All these phenomena happened by accident. Ancient Mayans in South America, finding their patterns behaving in mysterious ways, might have imagined the influence of gods or hallucinogenic 'magic' mushrooms.

After Sir David Brewster, the next name to be reckoned with is that of Bela Julesz, a perceptual psychologist employed by the Bell Telephone Company in the USA. In 1960 he developed the autostereogram's immediate forerunner, the computer-generated random-dot stereogram. Like the autostereogram, his idea made use of repetitive patterns concealed within screens of random dots. But, like a stereoscopic photograph, his picture was split into separate left and right images, which had to be viewed simultaneously. For all but the most skilled observers, who converge their eyes sufficiently to see them unaided, this still meant using lenses. On page 18 there are two pairs of diagrams. One illustrates the principle involved in the work of Julesz, while the other is a more practical example which, with practice, you may find you can view convergently with the naked eye.

Julesz's method was to make a random pattern of dots for one of the two images (the left or the right), then to copy it for the other eye. The copy, however, had one crucial difference from the original. Some regions of the pattern would be shifted a short distance horizontally, thus creating a subtle change of angle. This, as we have seen, is the essential ingredient for stereoscopic vision. The resulting image is 3-D.

For reasons which belong more properly to a scientific paper than to a book for the general reader, the effect of shifting the dots inward (i.e. towards the viewer's nose) is to make the image apparently float above the page. Regions of dots shifted outwards will appear to lie *behind* the plane of the page.

Random-dot stereograms, like the Wheatstone stereogram, mimic what happens in real life – feeding separate left/right images to the appropriate eye, which the brain then recombines into a 3-D picture. Because each random-dot image makes no sense on its own – there are no recognisable 'depth cues' for the eye to seize on, as there are in photographs – it provides a perfect method of testing for defects in binocular vision (though not, alas, of curing them).

The final breakthrough came in 1979 when an Englishman, Christopher Tyler, Associate Director of Smith-Kettlewell Eye Research Institute in San Francisco, produced the first true autostereogram. In many ways it was very like Julesz's random-dot stereogram. Again it relied on left/right images hidden in a field of random dots, but there was a very important difference. All the visual information necessary to create a 3-D image was contained *within a single frame*. The viewer could use both eyes together, and no longer needed the help of lenses or mirrors.

The principle was a sophisticated, highly-developed application of the Brewster 'wallpaper effect', relying on small, horizontally repeating patterns which merged into stereoscopic images. Unlike wallpaper, however, the autostereogram conceals its patterns within a screen of randomly scattered dots, while the widths of the repeating patterns could be varied to produce *varying* impressions of depth. Whereas the 'wallpaper effect' produces the illusion of a whole wall moving the same distance back or forward across its entire length, an autostereogram can produce an infinitely varied range of apparent depths – which means, in simple language, that you see it in three dimensions.

As the example on page 7 shows, the wider the pattern-repetition width, the greater the apparent change in depth. Pattern width of course also has a bearing on the distance from which an autostereogram can be viewed: the wider it is, the further away you will have to be to see it.

Tyler's real advantage over Brewster was to have lived in the age of the microchip. The precise degrees of 'shift' between the two images needed to produce the stereoscopic effect could be written into a computer program. Designs could be written into the program too, so that the patterns themselves no longer had to be random, but could be made to resemble real objects.

Tyler's first demonstration of autostereograms was in 1980, to

PAGE 20
Fish
Another early example that is very easy to 'see' and that can be viewed both ways (convergently and divergently). It is also a particularly good image on which to practise hypersight. There are four fishes, with two concave images and two convex images.
In hypersight, each of the images becomes multi-layered.

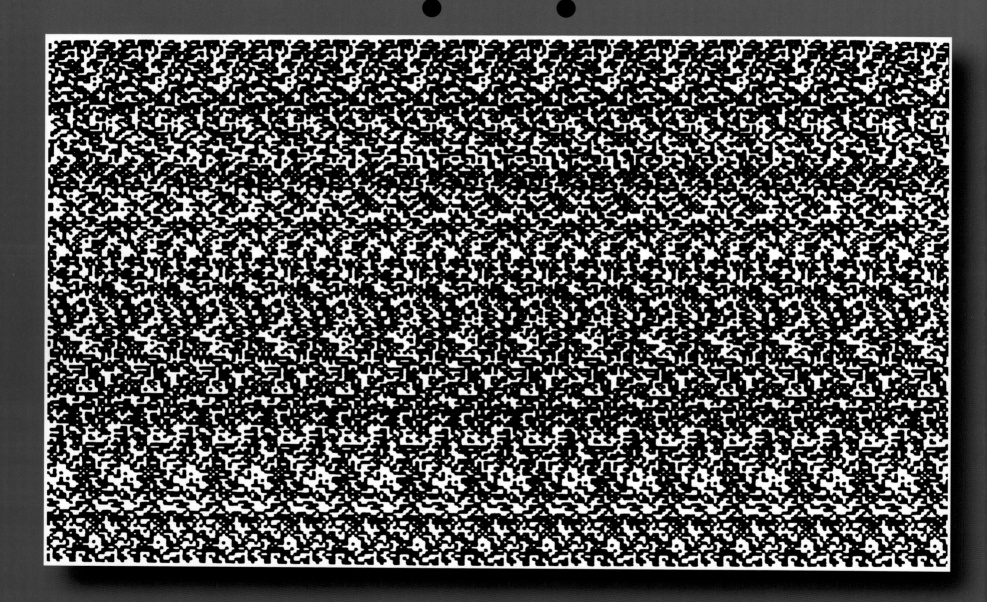

Example of simple stereograms showing viewing patterns

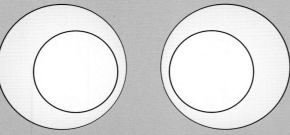

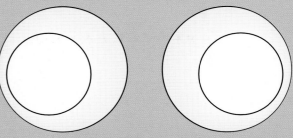

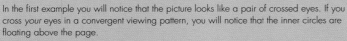

In the first example you will notice that the picture looks like a pair of crossed eyes. If you cross *your* eyes in a convergent viewing pattern, you will notice that the inner circles are floating above the page.

Holding the same convergent viewing pattern, and looking at the second example, you will notice that now the outer circle is floating above. This is a clear example of the meaning of 'Nasal Shift', and a clear demonstration of simple 3-D viewing.

a gathering of scientists at the US Association for Research in Vision and Ophthalmology. The first published example appeared in 1983. Early images included the heart, which we have already seen on page 15, the waves on page 21 and the staircase on page 23. In their original forms these, like most of the simpler dot-pattern examples, were in black and white only. Some later examples have been coloured especially for inclusion in this book.

The waves on page 21 show how an autostereogram grid is made up. All the computer does, of course, is to save a great deal of human time and trouble. If you like, you can easily design and make a simple autostereogram by hand. (See the examples above.)

In fact, the idea of producing left/right perspectives by hand is not a new one. The artist Salvador Dali tried it in his double image of the crucifixion, *Christ of Gala*, which hangs in the Museum Ludwig in Cologne. René Magritte's *L'Homme au Journal*, in the Tate Gallery, London, takes the idea even further, with two paired images – though you would need to be the ocular equivalent of an Olympic gymnast to make them 'read'!

It is no coincidence that both these painters were members of the Surrealist movement which flourished in the 1920s and 1930s and were influenced by the theories of Sigmund Freud. Surrealist painters lay great stress on the importance of dreams. Unreal or impossible images are depicted with great clarity and detail, giving them the intensity of nightmares. It is interesting – even a little disturbing – to speculate how these two artists might have responded had they been working 60 years later and with full awareness of the findings of Julesz and Tyler.

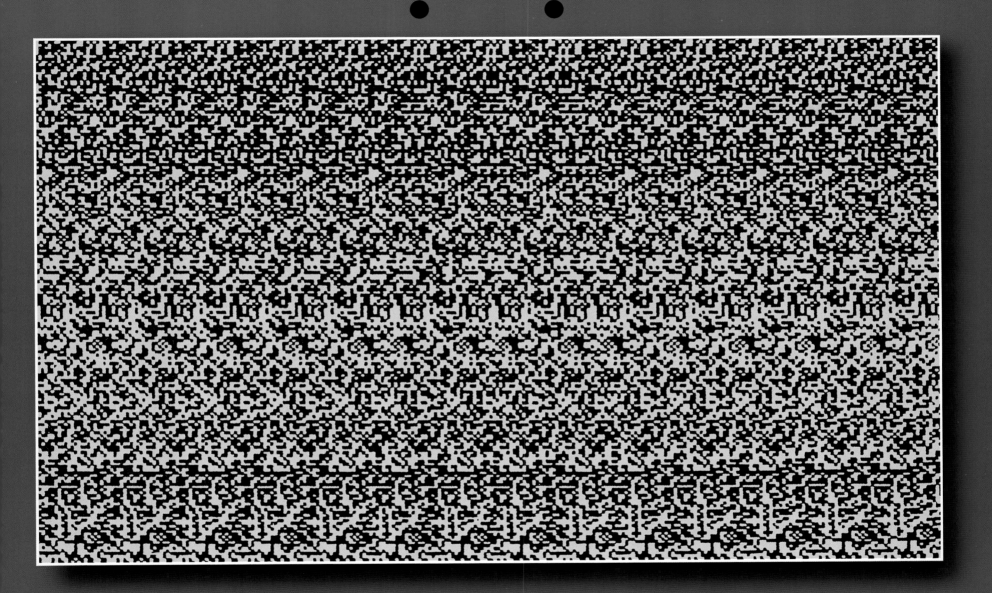

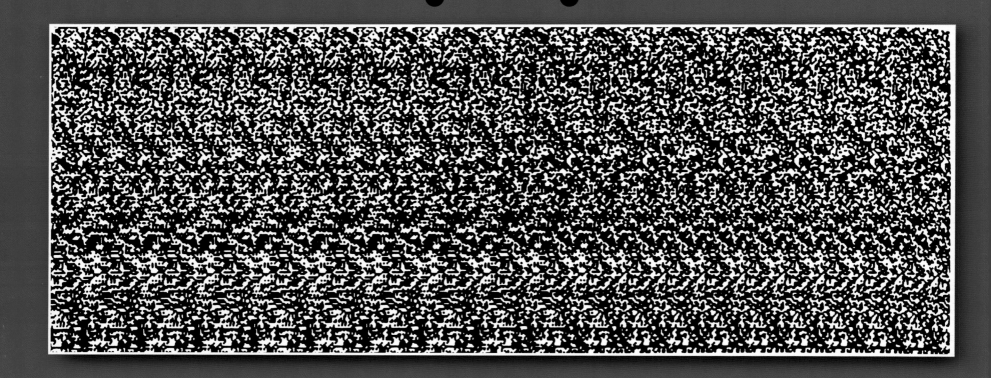

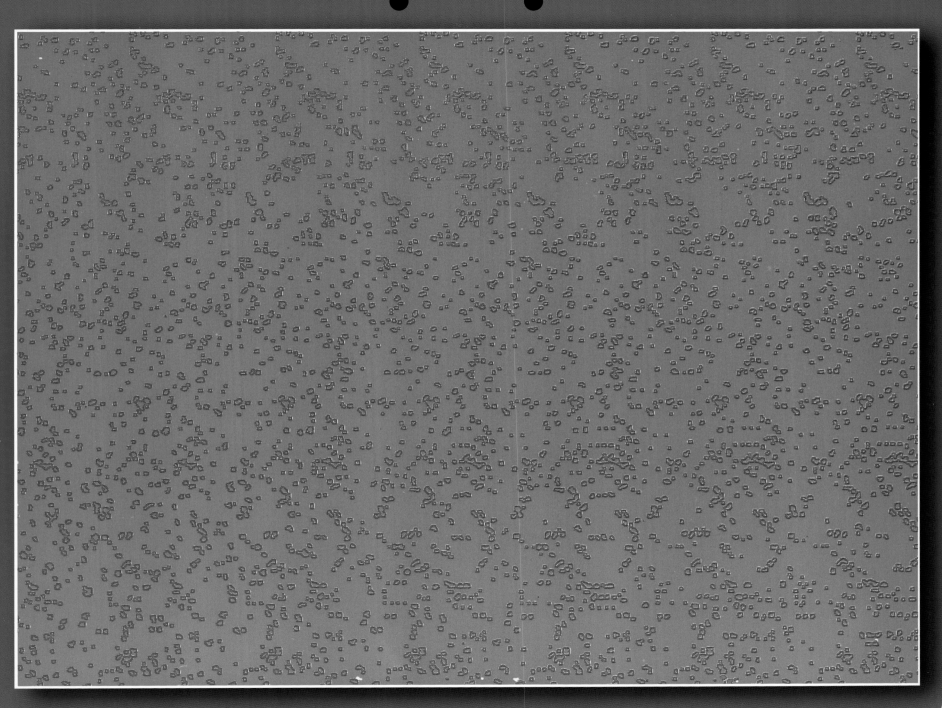

PAGE 25
Minimal Graphic
Another very early random dot autostereogram, showing how a fully realised three-dimensional image can be created from surprisingly little visual information. It may be viewed both convergently and divergently, although not everyone finds it easy to use.

PAGE 26
Tyres
This may be viewed both ways. The image reads as either an arrangement of car tyres standing on edge, or as slots in a toaster. When viewed convergently in hypersight, the tyres become increasingly narrower.

PAGE 27
Hexagons
This image, of six hexagons in a terraced dish, began life as a an ordinary random-dot stereogram. Computer processing has added colour and a sculptural edge, creating an image which in two dimensions looks remarkably like an abstract impressionist painting of a 12-layered flower-head sitting in a terraced bowl. Hypersight gives an interesting transformation when a 10-petalled flower emerges from the original flower, which now has eight sections.

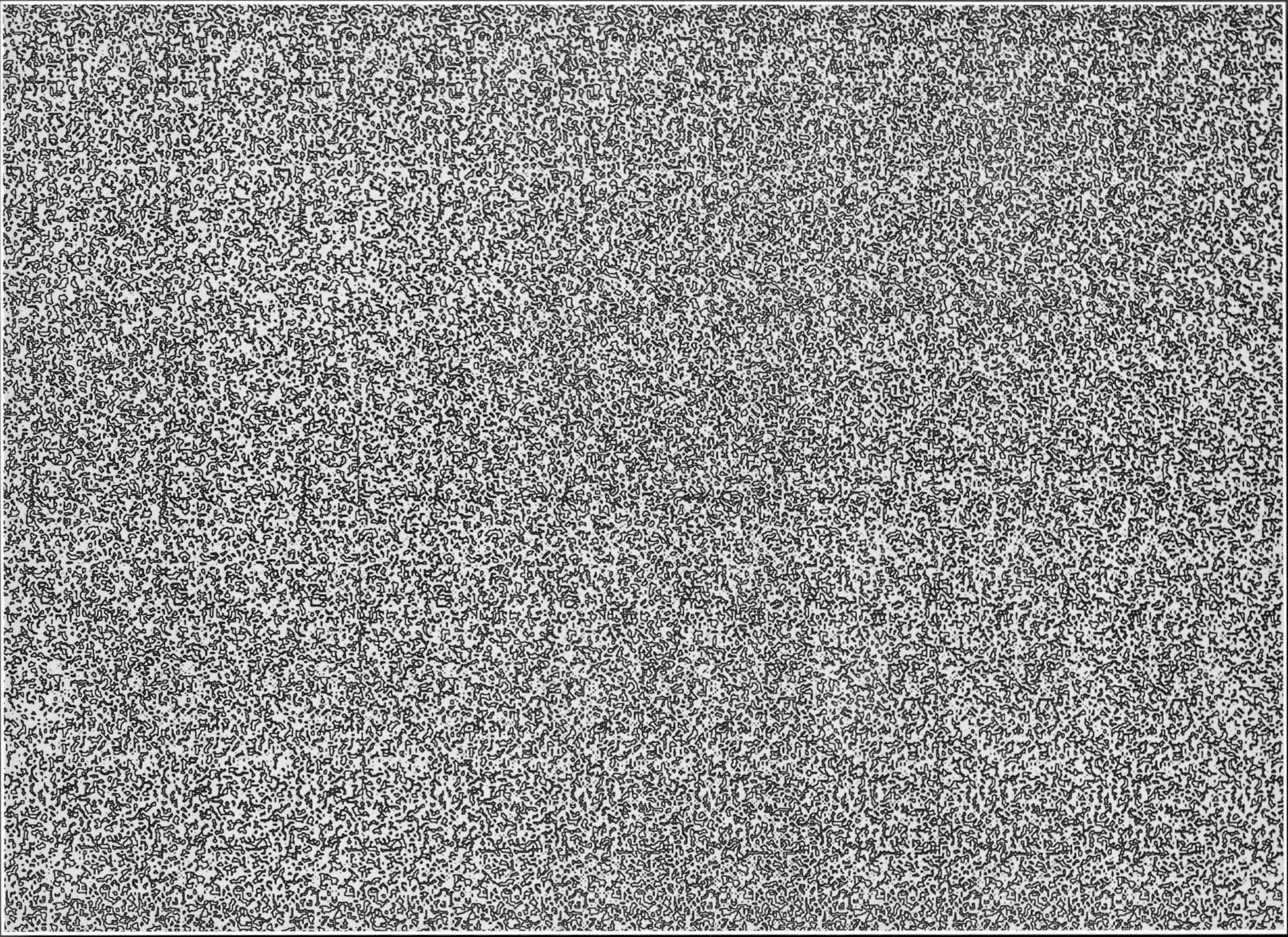

How to View an Autostereogram

Each autostereogram may be looked at in two different 'eye postures' – *convergent* and *divergent*. The latter does not mean that you have to make your eyes look in different directions simultaneously (that would be impossible), but only that you extend their point of focus.

> In convergent sight you must focus on a point
> *in front* of the image you want to see.

> In divergent sight you must focus on a point
> *behind* the image you want to see.

Some easy techniques for achieving both these modes of vision are described below. The length of time it takes to 'see' an autostereogram for the first time will vary from person to person. Some people may manage it immediately, and others will have to try for ten minutes or so before they find their point of focus. A few may take even longer. If you do have difficulty, then reassure yourself by trying the so-called 'Hot Dog Test'.

Make yourself comfortable in a well-lit room, then relax and allow yourself plenty of time. Concentration is required, so vocal encouragement from bystanders are (to put it mildly) unhelpful.

Hold your index fingers tip to tip but slightly apart, at eye level, horizontally, just in front of your nose. Focus your eyes through your fingers on a distant object in the room, and you will see the ghostly image of a third digit floating between your fingertips. Some people think it looks like a hot dog – hence the name. If you see it, then you'll be able to see an autostereogram. It's as simple as that.

VIEWING CONVERGENTLY

This is the basic method for viewing autostereograms, and for most people it is the easiest. You are training your eyes to focus on a point in front of the page. When you achieve the correct focus, the effect will be to make some of the images within the autostereogram appear to lift off the page towards you, while others will appear to descend.

Method 1 Hold the autostereogram on page 21 about 18 inches from your face. Stare at the two black dots printed at the top of the page. If you cross your eyes, the two dots appear to become four. Relax slightly, and they become three. Concentrate on the middle, imagined, dot and you will gradually become aware that something is starting to happen in the rest of your visual field – a mild disturbance followed by a gradual deepening of focus.

Slowly move your eyes from the dot, and you should have full 3-D vision. If you move your head from side to side, the images will appear to move with you. If you move gently backwards and forwards, the images will change in size.

Method 2 Again you should position the autostereogram about 18 inches from your face. This time ignore the dots but hold up a finger about 8-12 inches from your face. Focus hard – *stare* at the very tip of your finger. This will have the effect of making you go slightly cross-eyed – essential for making your eyes focus in the right plane. Very soon the autostereogram in the background will blur, or appear to move. When this happens, slowly take your finger away, *but without refocusing your eyes*, and the 3-D image should appear. A slight drawback of this method is the exact point of focus, indicated by the position of your finger, can only be found through trial and error.

Method 3 Many people find this method the easiest. Place your nose right against the centre of the autostereogram, cross your eyes and try to look at the tip of your nose. Keeping your eyes crossed, slowly move your nose away from the page. As soon as you reach the right focal length, the 3-D image will appear.

VIEWING DIVERGENTLY

Again, it must be emphasised that this method does not require you literally to 'diverge' your eyes, but rather to focus them on a point *behind* the autostereogram. Viewing divergently has the effect of reversing the images that you saw while viewing convergently. What appeared then to be above the surface, will now be below it, and vice versa. Some people find divergent sight harder to achieve than convergent, but the methods described below are both simple and reliable.

Method 1 Place a sheet of glass or clear plastic on top of the autostereogram. Stare at a reflection in the glass (e.g. your own), or a piece of white paper, while completely ignoring the printed pattern underneath. When the 3-D image appears, it will be as if you are peering down at it in a box. This will appear to become deeper or shallower as you move your head.

Method 2 This is similar to Method 3 for convergent sight, in that the starting position is with your nose touching the paper. This time, however, instead of crossing your eyes, you must stare straight ahead. Focus on the black random dots, or random coloured shapes, and imagine that they are far below the surface. There will be some

PAGE 43
Five Rows of Spheres
This is best viewed divergently, when the effect is like looking down on a plantation of trees that have been covered by a light dusting of snow. When viewed convergently, the spheres become indentations, or cups into which the spheres would fall.

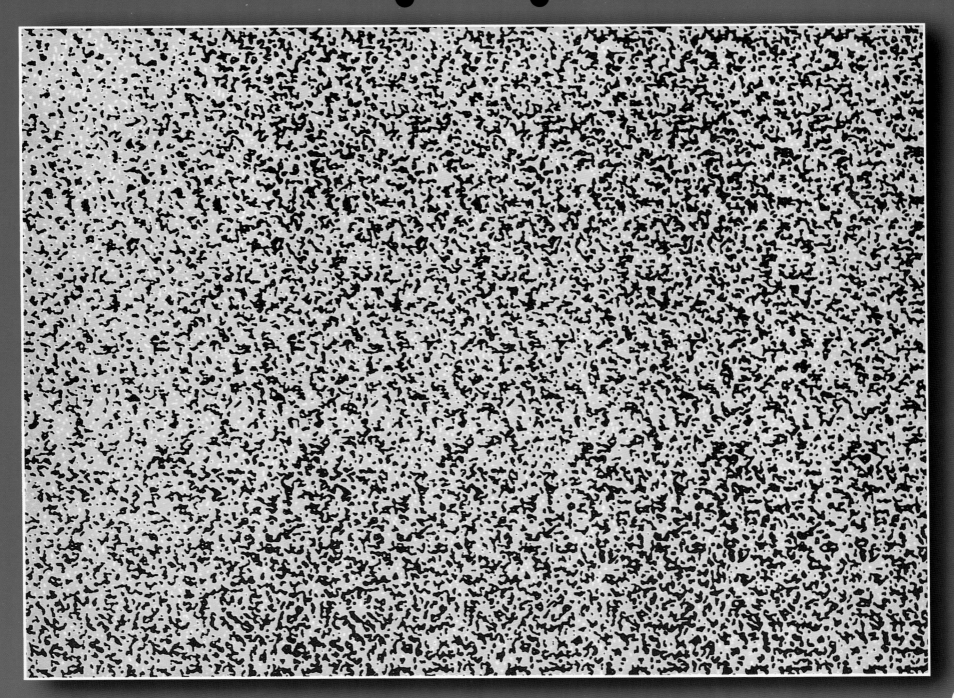

43

perturbation in the visual field while your eyes hunt for a focus, but quite quickly you should have the sensation of looking at the dots from a distance or through glass. Pull slowly back, and the 3-D image will appear.

HYPERSIGHT

This is the term used by enthusiasts to describe exaggerated forms of convergent and divergent vision, when the eyes are deflected by more than a single pattern width.

HYPERCONVERGENCE

This is easiest to achieve once your eyes are already convergently focused and you are seeing the image in 3-D. Without changing your focus, shift your eyes to the dots at the top of the page. (You should still be able to see three: two real and one imagined.) Cross your eyes and look at the tip of your nose again until the three dots become four. Now shift your gaze back to the autostereogram. You will see that the images are still basically recognisable, but they now appear smaller and more distant, as if you are looking through the wrong end of a telescope.

When you have mastered this technique, you can extend it still further by crossing your eyes again, and maybe again, until the four dots become six or eight. With this degree of convergence, the patterns will appear much more dense, and the images will begin to change their form. They will be both much smaller and greater in number than before.

Not everyone will see the dots multiply. Some will see only the original two pairs, but with an increasing degree of separation.

HYPERDIVERGENCE

For most people this is markedly more difficult to achieve. Again it is a question of extending the focus. Begin in regular divergent sight, then try to widen your focus to a point even further below the surface. As you might expect, you get precisely the reverse effect that you experienced with hyperconvergence. The images now appear much nearer, larger and fewer in number.

IMPROVING YOUR CONCENTRATION

You will find that your ability to 'hold' 3-D vision, either convergently or divergently, will greatly improve with practice. When you feel confident enough, you can further improve your capacity by exercising your eyes individually.

Once you have achieved stereoscopic focus, try closing one eye. The first few times you attempt this, the likeliest result is that the focus will immediately be lost. With time and practice, however, you should be able to retain focus in the open eye, and return to it with a closed eye as soon as you open it again. Eventually, you should be able to open and close your eyes alternately without ever losing focus. In time, your focus should become so assured that you will be able to close *both* eyes and return to convergent, divergent, or even hypervision when you reopen them.

PAGE 44
Deck of 14 Cards
This is best viewed divergently, and is good for hypersight. When viewed convergently, it looks like four staircases disappearing into the ground.

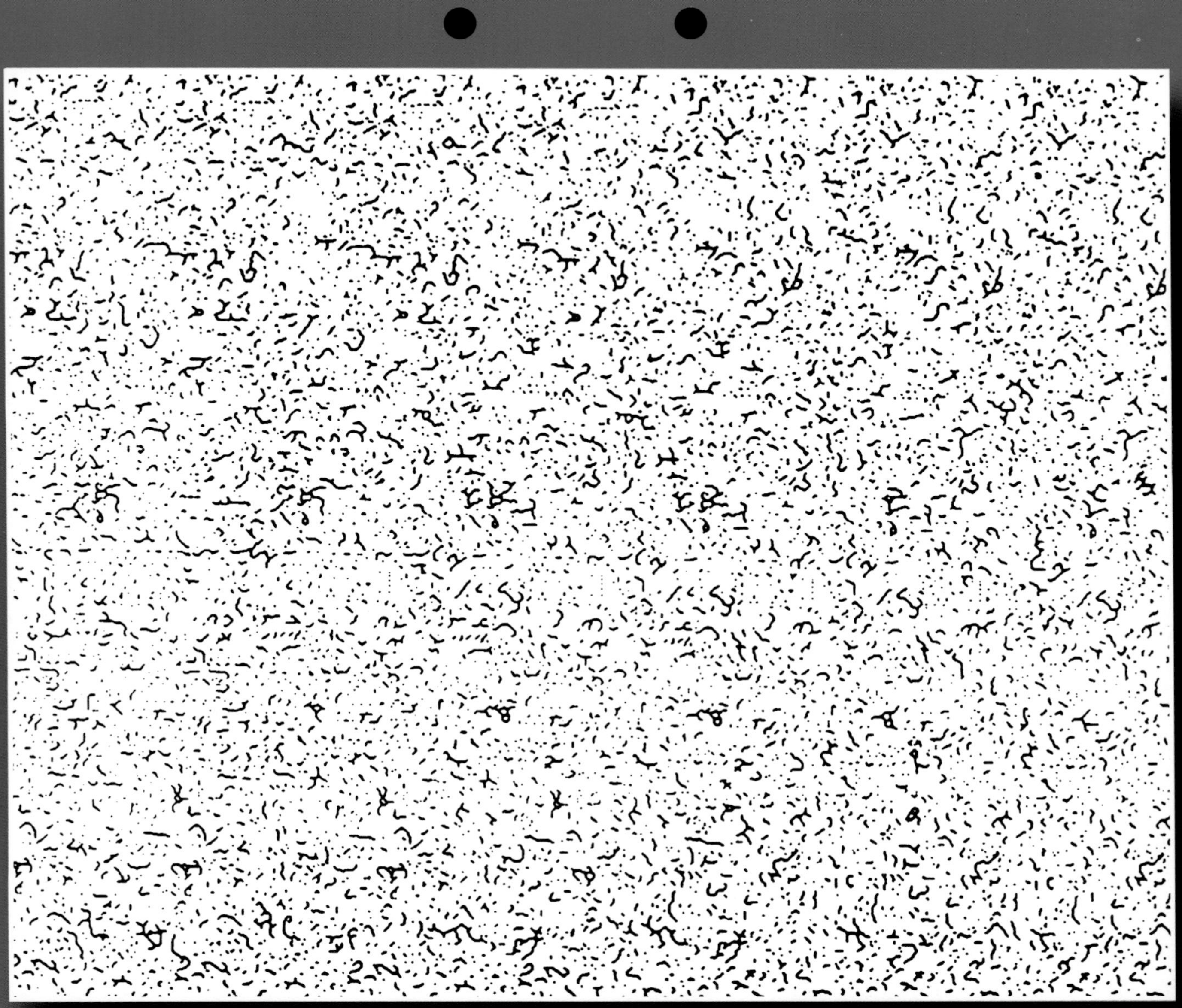

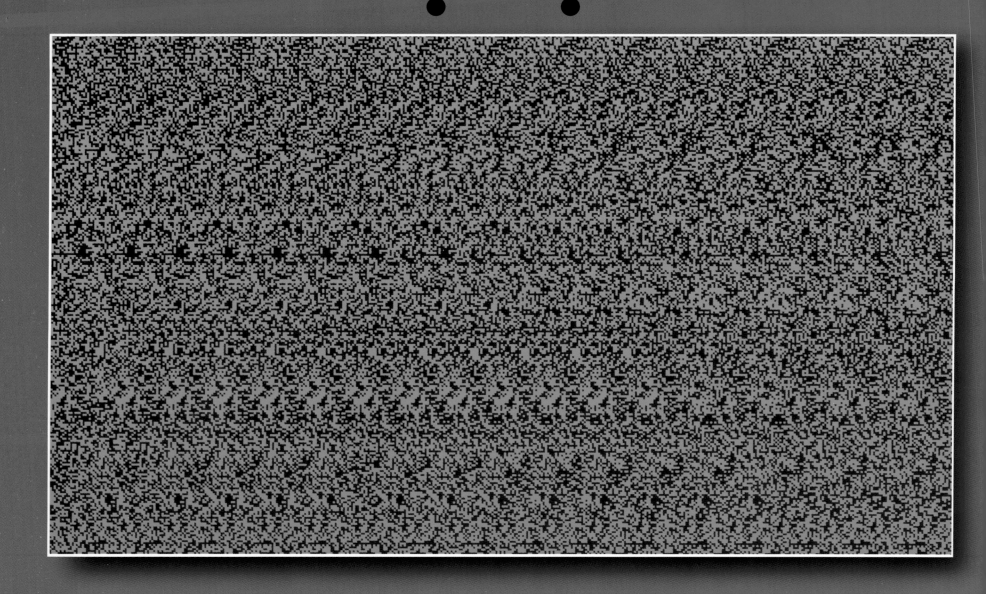

48

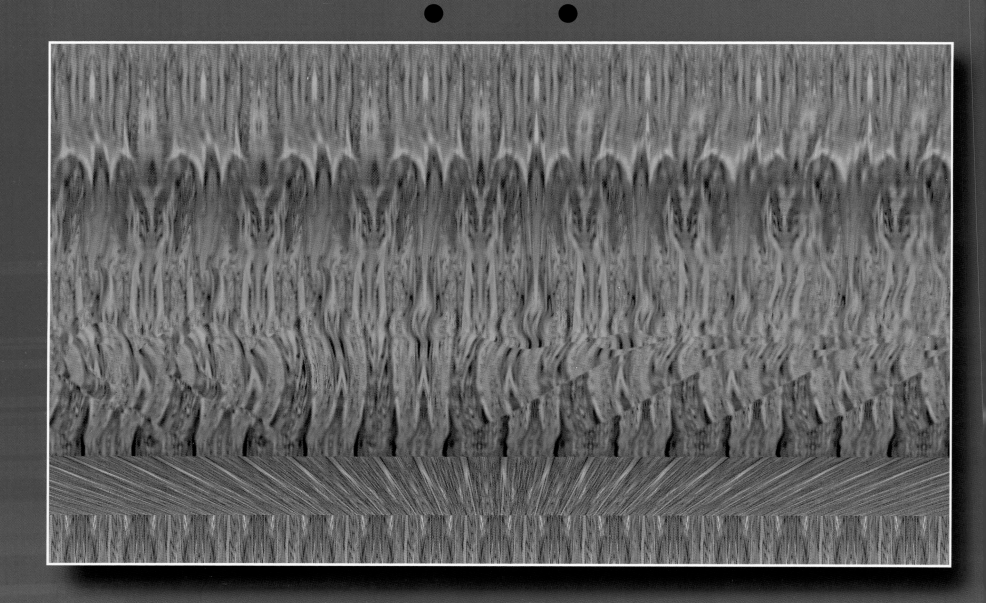

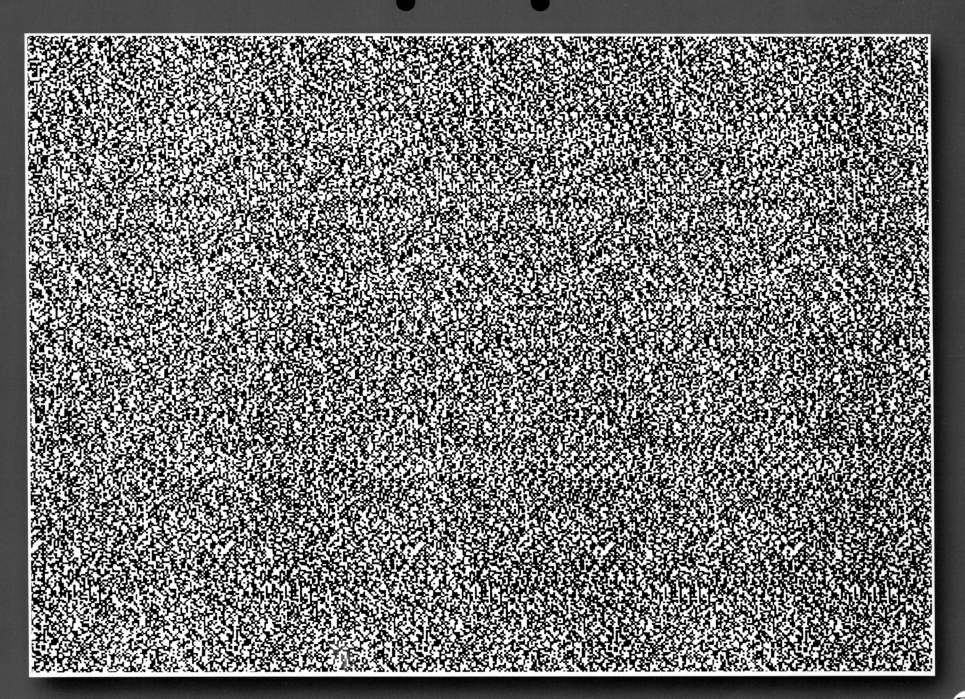

55

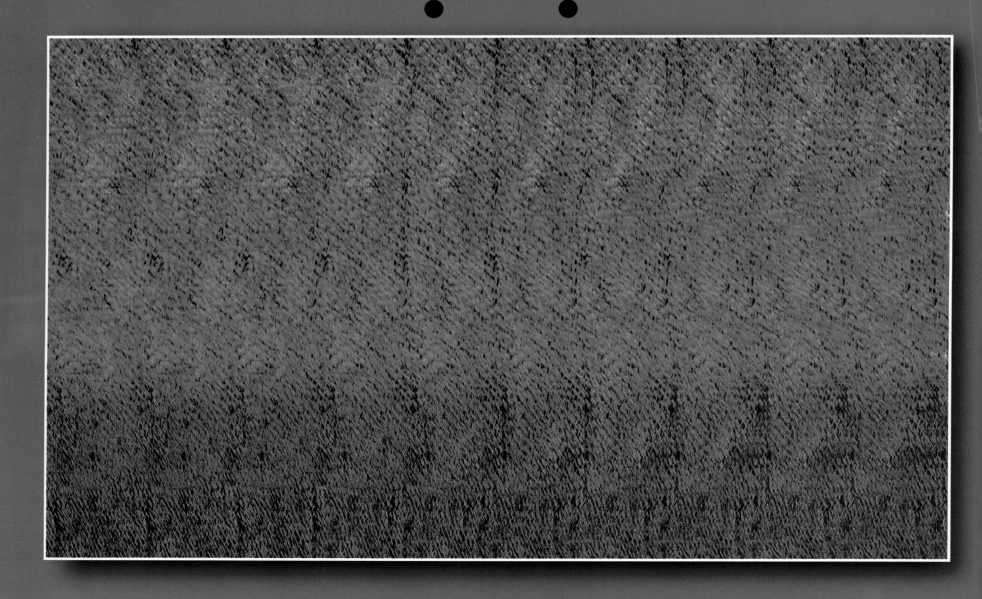

57

58